First Facts®

OUR GOVERNMENT

# THE CITY MAYOR

STEVE B. WILSON
MAYOR

BY JACK MANNING

CAPSTONE PRESS
a capstone imprint

First Facts are published by Capstone Press,
1710 Roe Crest Drive, North Mankato, Minnesota 56003
www.capstonepub.com

**Library of Congress Cataloging-in-Publication Data**
Cataloging information on file with the Library of Congress
ISBN 978-1-4914-0336-5 (library binding)
ISBN 978-1-4914-0340-2 (paperback)
ISBN 978-1-4914-0344-0 (eBook PDF)

**Editorial Credits**
Brenda Haugen, editor; Heidi Thompson, designer; Eric Gohl, media researcher;
Katy LaVigne, production specialist

**Photo Credits**
AP Photo: Rich Pedroncelli, cover, The Savannah Morning News/Richard Burkhart, 19;
Dreamstime: Jose Gil, 5; iStockphotos: EdStock, 13; Newscom: EPA/Erik S. Lesser, 9, MCT/Paul
Kitagaki Jr., 17, ZUMA Press/Bryan Smith, 21, ZUMA Press/Damaske, 15, ZUMA Press/Taylor
Jones, 1 (left); Shutterstock: Natalia Bratslavsky, cover (street sign), 1 (right), Semmick Photo, cover
(background), SoleilC, 7, Spirit of America, 11

Printed in the United States of America.
052018   000585

# TABLE OF CONTENTS

# CHAPTER 1

# CITY LEADERS

Can you imagine being in charge of a city the size of Los Angeles, California, or Dallas, Texas? You could if you were the mayor. In communities big and small, mayors serve as leaders.

Mayors have one of the most important jobs in city governments. A mayor leads the city in which he or she lives and works. The mayor meets with police officers and other important people in the community. The mayor talks to **citizens** about ideas for their cities. Together they work to make their cities better.

> **citizen**—a member of a country, state, or city who has the right to live there

# CHAPTER 2

# CITY GOVERNMENT

City governments are made of three parts. Mayors lead their communities. **City councils** pass new laws for the cities. Courts decide what laws mean.

Mayors look for ways to improve their cities. They write and sign laws to improve city **services** and keep people safe. They listen to citizens' ideas about many different **issues**.

**city council**—a group of people elected to look after the interests of a city
**service**—a system or way of providing something useful or necessary; city services include streets, water, and parks
**issue**—an idea or need that is talked about by citizens and government leaders

# CITY GOVERNMENT

## MAYOR

LEADS COMMUNITIES; WRITES AND SIGNS LAWS

## CITY COUNCIL

PASSES NEW LAWS

## COURT

DECIDES WHAT LAWS MEAN

# CHAPTER 3

# WHO CAN BE MAYOR

Not everyone can be a mayor. A **candidate** must follow rules to become mayor. The candidate must live in the city he or she wants to serve. The candidate also must be able to **vote** in that city. In some communities mayors must be at least 18 years old. In other cities mayors must be at least 21 years old.

candidate—a person who runs for office
vote—to make a choice in an election

# CHAPTER 4

# ELECTING MAYORS

Citizens vote for mayors to lead their communities. In some cities people **elect** mayors to serve two-year **terms**. In other places mayors serve four-year terms. When their terms are over, mayors may be elected again.

**elect**—to choose someone as a leader by voting
**term**—a set period of time that elected leaders serve in office

**FACT** In most U.S. communities, mayors can serve as many terms as they care to be elected to.

# CHAPTER 5

# A MAYOR'S JOB

Mayors work at city halls. At city hall a mayor plans projects for the community. The mayor makes sure the city has money to pay for services, such as police, parks, and water.

Mayors' days are often very busy. They meet with many people. They may talk with city workers about street repairs or building new parks. Mayors figure out ways to get the work done.

**FACT** Cities such as New York offer special homes or mansions where their mayors can live.

# CHAPTER 6

# CITY MANAGERS HELP MAYORS

City managers help mayors and councils with city business. A manager helps them plan how to spend a city's money. A manager helps plan projects to improve streets and keep the city's water clean.

A manager also helps hire people who work for the city. The manager makes sure city workers are doing their jobs well.

# CHAPTER 7

# WORKING WITH CITY COUNCILS

Mayors and city councils help make cities better places to live. They work together on new laws. They share ideas about city services. They talk about jobs, safety, and other issues. They work together to solve problems and improve their communities.

**FACT** The United States has about 19,000 cities, towns, and villages.

A mayor and city council listen to citizens and city workers at a meeting.

# CHAPTER 8

# SIGNING LAWS

Did you ever wonder who makes up the rules for your city? Maybe your city has laws saying how late you can play in your city's parks. The mayor and city council pass these laws to help keep citizens safe.

**FACT** In 1887 Susanna Salter of Argonia, Kansas, became the first female mayor in the United States.

TONY THOMAS
DISTRICT 6

EDNA B. JACKSON
MAYOR

Ideas for new laws often come from citizens. At meetings people talk with the mayor and council about plans for new laws. After listening to all sides of an issue, the mayor and council vote on the new law. In some cities mayors vote only when there is a tie. Mayors sign the new laws to make them official.

## Amazing but True!

Can you imagine having a dog as mayor? That's exactly what happened in a small California town. A black Labrador retriever named Bosco was elected mayor of Sunol, California. This small city had no real government. Some people thought it would be fun to name Bosco as the mayor. In one election Bosco got more votes than two other candidates. The dog served as mayor for 11 years.

Citizens who had ideas for a new law often watch the mayor sign the law and make it official.

# GLOSSARY

**candidate** (KAN-duh-date)—a person who runs for office

**citizen** (SIT-i-zuhn)—a member of a country, state, or city who has the right to live there

**city council** (SIT-ee KOUN-suhl)—a group of people elected to look after the interests of a city

**elect** (e-LEKT)—to choose someone as a leader by voting

**issue** (ISH-yoo)—an idea or need that is talked about by citizens and government leaders

**service** (SUR-viss)—a system or way of providing something useful or necessary; city services include streets, water, and parks

**term** (TERM)—a set period of time that elected leaders serve in office

**vote** (VOHT)—to make a choice in an election

# READ MORE

**Hoffman, Mary Ann**. *I Am a Good Citizen*. Kids of Character. New York: Gareth Stevens, 2011.

**Jakubiak, David J**. *What Does a Mayor Do?* How Our Government Works. New York: PowerKids Press, 2010.

**Jeffries, Joyce**. *Meet the Mayor*. People Around Town. New York: Gareth Stevens Publishing, 2014.

# INTERNET SITES

FactHound offers a safe, fun way to find Internet sites related to this book. All of the sites on FactHound have been researched by our staff.

Here's all you do:

Visit *www.facthound.com*

Type in this code: 9781491403365

# INDEX

## CRITICAL THINKING USING THE COMMON CORE

1. Mayors lead their cities, but they get a lot of help. Who helps mayors? How do they help mayors? (Key Ideas and Details)
2. Mayors write and sign laws to improve their cities. If you were mayor, what law would you write to make your community better? Say why. (Integration of Knowledge and Ideas)